Narcissism

Confronting A Narcissist With Confidence After Escaping A Codependent Relationship

(How To Recover From Narcissistic Ex-partners And Parents In Order To Co-Parent)

Fernando Roberson

TABLE OF CONTENT

How to Deal with Narcissistic Coworkers 18

Be A Good Employee.. 21

The Narcissist's Equipment... 33

Be wary of the Flying Monkey. 48

Start the Healing Process and Regain Your Confidence and Self-Esteem 77

Chapter 5: Methods for Handling a Narcissistic Mother 110

The In-Law's Narcissistic Mother................................. 123

Conclusion... 139

Chapter 6: Retrieve Your Life.. 142

How to Frequently Say No.. 157

How Should I Approach the Narcissist in My Relationship? 173

Self-love is not the same as self-preservation. Self preservation compels you to apply moisturizer to your skin so that it does not crack from dehydration. Self preservation compels you to take a bath, as germs will kill you if you don't. However, it baffles me that crazed men who don't bathe for years are still alive, and I don't understand how children can consume sand without getting sick.

This is the paradox of the narcissist: he or she is filled with self-hatred and self-loathing. The suffering they inflict on others is a reflection of their own emptiness. They are unable to fill the void, so they lash out at everyone.

There are conflicting accounts of how narcissism develops, but the majority agree that it begins in infancy. Everyone born as an infant is entirely dependent on parents or caregivers, and crying is the only way to get them to do what the infant desires. The baby cries, the parents/caregivers scramble to meet the child's needs, and the child begins to believe that the parent has no existence outside of the child's sphere because the parent is constantly present. At some point, however, we are expected to make the transition when we become self-aware as individuals and allow our parents to become their own people. Then we begin to grow and become independent as we begin to separate from one another.

Typically, narcissism develops during childhood due to neglect or maltreatment. So the individual decides, "Since nobody cares about me, nobody pays attention to me, and everyone is being cruel and unkind to me, I'll just create my own world and stay in it, and I'll deal with anyone who tries to approach me." It is an unconscious process. In a sense, the narcissist needs compassion and sympathy because he or she is a person who failed to mature. They are incapable of loving their true self because they despise themselves; consequently, they fall in love with their own reflection, which is a false self. One of the cunning characteristics of the narcissist is the ability to mirror others. If he encounters you today and you are a pastor, oh, he will start a conversation with you in order to pick your brain and collect all the scriptures you like. When he meets you again, he will quote the same verses back to you, and you will be astounded. We share so many similarities! This is how he wins you over. If you inform him that you are a musician, he will respond, "Oh, I play the piano a bit." You inquire, "Can we jam sometime?" Indeed, he will respond. But every time you attempt to terminate the session, he will be unavailable; he lied to you because he does not play the keyboard. They mirror everyone they encounter. Therefore, when you first meet a narcissist and he looks at you, likes you, and believes you can contribute something to his life, he pursues you and says, "I want you to be my girlfriend." What you receive is known as love bombardment. Their capacity to 'love' rapidly and unexpectedly is astounding. Within a couple of months of meeting someone, they may propose matrimony. Quickly. Please take a step back from anyone in a relationship who behaves in this manner. They are eager to ensnare you and incorporate you into their lives so that you cannot escape.

Moreover, guess what? The narcissist always targets lovely people, also known as empaths, because they will be bitten if they approach another narcissist. It will fail. Consequently, you typically discover that narcissists are wedded to the kindest individuals. To be clear, there are both masculine and female narcissists. Female narcissists cause more devastation than male narcissists because you would not expect a woman to be a narcissist.

So they rush you into the relationship, leaving you no time to reflect: they marry you swiftly, quickly, quickly.

As you read, you may realize certain truths about yourself and/or your relationships. The narcissist is able to generate the much-needed narcissistic supply, also known as 'fuel', by projecting the image that he or she mirrors you and knows you. They require this supply like a car requires gasoline to function. The term "narcissistic supply" refers to whatever fuels the narcissist's defenses, regardless of whether it is a primary or secondary source. Please elucidate the meaning of these two terms.

Everyone around the narcissist will serve as propellant for him or her. He may obtain petroleum from the traffic officer. Let him simply drive by, and as soon as the warden greets or acknowledges him, he will receive fuel.

This is a secondary source due to the distance between the two parties. He can derive inspiration from the people in his office, including the cleaner, messenger, and security guard. He is the one who can go around and tip the subordinate staff with small amounts of money, so that when he returns to the office, they will revere him. He is not motivated by altruism, compassion, or benevolence; rather, he is interested in gaining something from them.

The primary source is the individual with whom the narcissist has a direct relationship. They desire this person's energy the most. The principal source is not permitted to leave the narcissist. If a companion escapes from a narcissist, the narcissist is capable of murdering or acid-attacking the individual. If I cannot have you, then no one else can. You are my source of supply; you have no right to discard or discard me. You must remain here until your death" For the narcissist, it is truly till death do us part, even after divorce, not from a position of the marriage vow, but from a mindset of "I am not letting you go until I kill you"; they do not release or let go of the person.

If you were previously in a relationship with a person who has continued to antagonize you after you ended the relationship, you should contact the police. You may loose your life because they will not release you. This was the motivation behind the assassination of some individuals. Narcissists don't let go.

Permit me to say a few words about the fuel. If they do not receive fuel, it is as if everything they have constructed on the inside is disintegrating. Therefore, they must acquire petroleum from wherever they can. The fuels have varying quality ratings. When you visit a gas station, you will typically see advertisements for both leaded and unleaded fuel. Unleaded gasoline costs more than leaded. Fuels for the narcissist are categorized. The fuel he receives from the secondary supply is of poor quality, so it won't do him much good. However, the one he obtains from the primary source is the most potent, so he injures it the most. The fuel they obtain from kindness is of inferior quality than the fuel they obtain from nastiness. For instance, if he wakes up and dresses nicely in the morning, and his spouse tells him, "You look great!"

Unlike most couples, Melanie and I were able to settle our divorce swiftly. Melanie was responsible for paying me a sum of money because she had more assets than I did at the conclusion of the transaction.

Melanie wasn't liquid. For convenience, she would pay me over four years as my company stock options matured. This was acceptable, as I was not in need of money.

We were pleased with the settlement, and now that it had been reached, I could sense the tension between us diminishing. Considering what we had been through, I was no longer furious.

I was more than anything else relieved.

We had a flexible arrangement for shared custody. It was essential because we both had hectic work seasons, and Melanie often had to work late during the week, while I had to work primarily on the weekends.

I had recently moved into an apartment in my homeland and was beginning to find my footing. I invested the divorce settlement and within no time had more than multiplied the amount.

Melanie and I only communicated when one of us became stranded. Melanie was treating the children as she always had, which was to pamper them. She had performed the character admirably. A month had passed, and everything was going swimmingly. I had an event scheduled for the weekend that the kids were off, so I called Melanie to trade weekends. She became extremely stern and informed me that she would not transfer and that we needed to stick to our schedule. As this was the first time I had requested a switch, I found it strange that she had responded with such a hostile tone. It was also approaching her busy season, so I anticipated that my phone would ring frequently if she stayed the night in New York City for business. I said OK, no concerns, I got it.

She then stated, "Child support is due on the seventh and no later." Now I consistently paid child support, but never on the same day.

Melanie did not require it, and I have always been lenient, but something was amiss. This was not the Melanie I had known for the majority of my adulthood. I waited a few days before calling her back. This time, it was to discuss my mother's schedule. Melanie had employed my mother to get the children off the bus, feed them, and get them ready for bed because she worked in New York City. Once again, I encountered a hostile attitude. I eventually paused and said, "Hey!" How are things? She responded, "Everything is in order. Why are you inquiring? The past week and a half, Melanie, you have been a bit short-tempered and rude towards me. Why don't I understand? She responded, "Well, I have an existence, and I can't keep switching things around and destroying it.

And you must make timely child support payments. It is the law. I took a deep breath and stated, "Look, I am willing to collaborate with you for the benefit of our children. You are approaching your busy season, and both you and I are aware that there will be several evenings in which I will be responsible for the children. I have no complaints. It would be simple for me to express. No, but I'm also aware that you tend to overwork under pressure, so I'm exerting great effort to make this work. Each of us pledged the other that we would collaborate. Please inform me if this has changed, and we'll be like every other divorced couple. She paused for a moment before saying, "You know, you're correct, I've been under a lot of stress recently, and this is a difficult adjustment. I'm sorry. I want to find a solution with you." I agreed that we could work together and instructed her to contact me if she becomes blocked.

Things appeared to stabilize. A week later, I was at my mother's house with the children. They were viewing television in the living room, while I spoke with my mother in the kitchen. I told her about the incident with Melanie from the previous week and asked her if she had noticed a difference. My mother stated that she hadn't. Tess entered the kitchen to get a pretzel and a drink while we were conversing. After opening the refrigerator, she turned to us and said, "Rock was lamenting about his mother switching weekends, and why is she always so accommodating with you? Rock believes that you and your mother should be typical divorced parents. Tess left the room to return to viewing television, at which point I turned to my mother and said, "Well, Rock can kiss my ass." We each laughed.

How to Deal with Narcissistic Coworkers

Ientered the career world with a high degree of naiveté. In my mind, if a group of people could plan, organize, and execute to the point that they form a working organization, they must be highly intelligent and surely have mastered the art of human interaction. This line of thinking led to a large amount of trust toward individuals who were simply- desperately- trying to fill a role. I would buy in to the mission vision values chat with wild enthusiasm. I would walk in with high expectations and almost always be let down.

The sobering reality is companies inflate their "resume" to prospective employees just as much as prospective employees exaggerate their skills and abilities. It's not just one-sided. When companies do it, it is often to hide an undercurrent of dysfunction they hope the potential employee doesn't pick up on in the interview. That undercurrent is often tainted with narcissistic individuals in positions of influence.

The Solution: Ask as many questions as you can in the interview process. Questions like, "Is this a new position or am I replacing someone? Were they promoted or have they left the company? What is your vision for the next three years for this department? What is the turnover rate? What is the average tenure here?" You are trying to get an idea of what they're not telling you, so you can make an informed decision. Companies with little to hide will have no problem having this discussion with you. Make sure to take advantage of review websites like Glassdoor and CareerBuilder.

Be A Good Employee

Nothing attracts narcissists more than the delicious nectar of a genuinely competent employee. You adhere to the rules to the best of your knowledge and ability, you have a high level of integrity, you produce quality work products, and worst of all, people like you. Why then would this be a survival tip? Because you must identify the narcissists.

Non-narcissistic entities (NNEs) will not perceive your outstanding performance as a threat. In contrast, they will be drawn to it and attempt to build it up, cultivate it, and promote it. NNEs are extremely concerned with the success of the business and are aware that exceptional performers contribute to that success. They do not endeavor to "bring that individual down" because it is illogical and counterintuitive. In contrast, narcissists are only concerned with personal victory. In order to maintain their perceived power position, they must extinguish any emerging star.

To entice narcissists out of their holes, the solution is to be the finest employee possible. Once identified, you will be in a much better position to avoid entanglements, although this is not always feasible. At the very least, you can maintain a professional distance and share only business-related information.

Maintain A Career Journal

Deep relationships with narcissists will almost always necessitate recalling past events. They have a unique ability to distort reality, especially the past. If you have direct contact with narcissists at work, such as a supervisor, you will need to document your daily activities and conversations in anticipation for inevitable "showdowns."

This may seem tedious, but it is more tedious to need the information in six months and not have it. Even worse is being face-to-face with a narcissist and having no idea what to say. Your mind will be liberated by the knowledge that everything is carefully stored for future reference. You should also make a point to record every compliment, commendation, honor, and recognition you receive at work. This will serve as a reminder and evidence of the quality of your work.

The Treatment: There are numerous simple methods to maintain a career journal:

Send yourself a summary via email at the conclusion of each day.

2. Use a daily planner with a bulleted list format.

Utilize the voice recorder on your smartphone to record one-minute daily summaries. Perform this while riding home from work.

Determine Your True Desires

It is much simpler for narcissistic people to exert control over you if you lack a clear sense of purpose. When you lack a firm grasp on your own objectives, you become susceptible to their suggestions and manipulative methods. It is much simpler to become "caught up." In light of this, it is essential that you determine what you hope to gain from this particular working situation.

What is more important: money or experience? Are you working for this employer solely for the compensation? If so, your situation becomes much simpler to escape, as money is abundant.

Determine your true purpose for being there and plan accordingly. If money is the only factor, increase your exit fund and exit as soon as feasible. If it's the experience you're after, devise a plan to acquire as much or as many as possible as quickly as possible. This clarity will aid in guiding your actions and preventing narcissism.

Define Personal Boundaries Within Organizational Policies

Every business has guidelines. Some rules make logic, while others do not, but may be necessary for you to maintain your position. When you establish boundaries within company policy, you determine when and where you can be yourself, as well as what "being yourself" means in that particular workplace.

For instance, participation in after-hours gatherings and group excursions is an unspoken expectation in many workplaces. Obviously, if this is part of what you are required to do for pay, you must do it. However, if it's not part of your job description and it's not something you typically or instinctively do, you should carefully consider whether this is a territory you wish to restrict. Boundaries are merely you maintaining your own integrity. If you enjoy happy hours and mingling with colleagues, you would not naturally erect a boundary because this is innately 'you.'

Burnout is the result of not identifying and protecting your boundaries. You end up giving away bits and parts of yourself until you are almost unrecognizable. Yes, to this and this as well. Yes, yes, yes until you are totally exhausted. This leaves you in a state of extreme vulnerability and desperation, which increases your likelihood of falling for narcissistic pitfalls and manipulations by a factor of ten.

Prior to accepting a job offer, you should make every effort to determine the rule system in force. Some individuals favor companies with a strong organizational structure. Some do not. Choose an environment that complements your natural disposition. It's not always simple to predict the type of environment you'll be in, so once you arrive, you should begin to establish company policy boundaries. You may irritate some individuals, but only those with narcissistic traits will be genuinely offended.

How to Deal with Narcissists at Work

Workplace narcissists cause significant suffering and create havoc. As with so many unfavorable circumstances in life, avoiding this difficult situation is the best course of action. Unfortunately, it may be impossible to avoid, as none of us has complete influence over who we work with and who is hired in a corporate setting.

Identifying a narcissist is typically not difficult. As long as you remain vigilant for these individuals throughout your career, you can avoid becoming a victim. As mentioned previously, a narcissist's inflated ego, sense of accomplishment, and inability to accept criticism are the most telling characteristics. A significant proportion of business owners and corporate executives are narcissists.

Here are some strategies for working with narcissists.

Never criticize a narcissist. When providing them with much-needed feedback, it is essential to express the facts without implying anything negative about what they have said or done. You must approach sensitive topics with a monotone tone to spare them any potential disgrace. Whenever there is a possibility that they might feel embarrassed, it is best to have this conversation in private.

Create reasonable restrictions. One of the issues that always arises when interacting with individuals with this personality disorder is their lack of boundaries. They may expect you to accept a call at 11 p.m. or have no problem with you working during the birth of your child. Unless you want to give up any semblance of a personal life, it is essential to establish your boundaries early on in a friendly yet firm manner. The narcissist will continue to challenge your limits. Keep in mind that the narcissist will typically back off if you adhere to your decision and are nice.

Establish a contingency plan in the event that you are forced to resign or fired with short notice. Everything is conceivable when working with a narcissistic supervisor or coworker. Even if you do a fantastic job, you are still at risk.

Do not anticipate gratitude or appreciation from a narcissistic supervisor or colleague. Your contributions and achievements are likely to go unrecognized, and the narcissist will frequently claim credit for them. Keep your calm in this situation, keeping in mind that narcissists manipulate others.

Do not reveal any intimate information that could be used against you to a narcissist. Personal information should be avoided at all costs when interacting with this personality type.

Calm your emotions by remembering that narcissists are frequently unhappy people who grew up in dysfunctional families. They will not specifically target you unless you humiliate them in some fashion. They utilize everyone to advance themselves, so it is impersonal.

The Narcissist's Equipment

Narcissists project a powerful, overconfident, and self-centered image that can quickly spiral out of control. This is malignant narcissism, the type that leads to despair when the narcissist cannot get their way or is forced to examine their own weaknesses. To avoid this, the malignant narcissist will go to great lengths and occasionally engage in preposterous behavior.

They will appear to be arrogant and above the law. They will project a superiority complex and imply that everyone else is inferior in some way. As soon as their lack of empathy becomes apparent, they lose all of their initial popularity.

Nature or Nurture

During infancy, we have a completely devoted caregiver who regards us as the center of the universe, giving us the impression that we are all-powerful and capable of achieving anything we desire. Typically, as we mature, we begin to realize that we are distinct from our caregiver, shedding these preconceived notions and establishing trust as we discover that our caregivers are distinct individuals, establishing boundaries, and eventually experiencing push-back in response to our demands and actions. This process establishes a healthy ego and initiates the development of realistic and mutually beneficial mature relationships.

Narcissists do not undergo this development. Typically, this occurs when the caregiver cannot handle the responsibility of providing comprehensive care for another individual. They never develop trust in their caregivers and never realize that they are not all-powerful and cannot exert control over others. Instead, they persist in their infantile belief that they are the center of the universe and manipulate those around them to maintain this position.

Manipulation

When interacting with a narcissist, you must anticipate at least some manipulation. They are attention addicts who are intent on protecting their vulnerable inner self, which translates to pressuring or coercing others to give the narcissist the attention they crave, to live up to their vision, and most importantly, to refrain from doing anything that might force them to admit that their inflated self-image is inaccurate.

They could care less if the people they manipulate suffer as a result. Their belief is that it is impossible to create an omelet without breaking some eggs. If the person they are manipulating pushes back, resists the manipulation, and forces the narcissist to confront their own ugliness, the narcissist's response is typically violent, if not physically so, then intense and frequently venomous. They may malign the individual, blame them for the narcissist's own actions, or degrade them in order to intimidate them into silence.

A narcissist employs a wide variety of manipulation techniques. Some can be quite delightful, others are subtle, and the remainder are repulsive. They may be used individually or in combination, and will be modified as necessary for the narcissist to attain their objectives. Based on how the subject is made to feel, we have divided these techniques into three categories: The Good, the Bad, and the Ugly.

The (not quite) Good Love-bomb Their Partner. The victim has never in their life felt so adored. The narcissist will do this to swiftly hook and reel in their victim. The narcissist does not wish for them to reflect, examine what is occurring closely, or ask numerous inquiries.

They admire their partner. They create a fictitious ideal of their victim and then treat them as if they actually meet that ideal. As with love bombing, this can be quite pleasant for the victim until the narcissist turns on them, which occurs when the reality of a relationship settles in and they begin to see flaws in their partner that they wish to change or eliminate.

Subtle Compliment. This early-stage tactic, like idealization, opens the door to other things by making the partner feel good about themselves and the narcissist, good enough to enable the narcissist greater access to their life.

Replicating Their Partner. In the beginning, narcissists are interested in their partner's tastes, values, and beliefs in order to mirror them and make them believe they've found the perfect match. However, once the narcissist achieves the love of their love object, their interest and attention typically wane.

The Poor

The Victim's Role. The narcissist plays the victim on purpose to elicit the sympathy of the person being manipulated, often hosting the pity party of the century to induce them to act.

The Game of Obligation. The Narcissist's penchant for tit-for-tat and their ability to manipulate our sense of fairness come to the forefront when they do something good to obligate someone to do something for them, sometimes against the other person's self-interest.

Making Excuses. Slightly distinct from the narcissist's victim play, they are attempting to justify or excuse their behavior by deflecting responsibility and eliciting the pity of the abused party. "If I had only received the money I'm owed" or "If you had simply kept your promise not to...", the narcissist is always the victim in these excuses. In any relationship, the last thing a narcissist desires is for their companion to have expectations of them. By lowering these expectations, a gradual process of diminishing returns in which the partner becomes accustomed to receiving less and less from the narcissist, they end up expecting little or nothing from the relationship while the narcissist continues to extricate what they desire.

Gambling on Hope. In and of itself, lowering expectations is a surefire method to destroy any relationship. They eventually recognize there is no point in continuing and move on. Since the narcissist derives sustenance from their companion, this is the very last thing they desire. Therefore, like any effective parasite, they must find a balance between feeding off their host and killing them. To accomplish this, the narcissist will occasionally turn on the charm and be everything their partner desires in order to weaken their defenses and give them something to cling to when their normal behavior reemerges.

The Treatment of Silence. The narcissist is not always successful. Their companion may say or do something to penetrate their defenses. They may have merely declined a request. The response is anger. Occasionally, this is expressed verbally or physically, and occasionally, the narcissist ceases interacting with their partner. This type of bullying behavior is intended to sow seeds of doubt and ambiguity in the partner's mind. The objective is to keep them puzzled and anticipating the next move.

Word Play. The narcissist manipulates the partner's perception of reality. This takes the extreme form of gaslighting, which we will discuss below. On the more benign end of the spectrum, they use words to confuse, demean, and degrade their victim, often asserting that they are "joking" or "misspoke."

The Unattractive Devaluation. The narcissist can undermine their partner's self-esteem through word games. They accomplish this by intentionally saying, not saying, and doing, or not doing, things that devalue the victim. Nothing about this behavior could be construed as a joke or a mistake; it is overt and personal, ranging from ignoring an accomplishment to questioning their clothing preference to comparing them unfavorably to others. In addition to making the narcissist feel good about themselves, the goal is to make their partner feel as though they do not deserve superior treatment.

Refute everything and demand evidence. When the victim confronts the narcissist about their behavior, the typical response is denial and demands for proof, which are then contorted to either excuse the behavior or place the blame on the victim (see Gaslight Is More Than a Movie, Below).

The Game of Triangulation. In order to assert control, the narcissist introduces other people into the relationship in order to anger and provoke jealously in the victim. This could be a person the narcissist uses as an example to demean their partner, or someone who supports or even aids the narcissist (see Beware the Flying Monkey).

Developing Guilt. Similar to the stereotypical Jewish mother, the narcissist will use remorse as a weapon. The goal is to deflect responsibility for their behavior and break down resistance by convincing the partner that the problems between them and the narcissist are their fault, thereby rendering them vulnerable and more willing to comply with the narcissist's unreasonable demands.

Bullying. When confronted with blowback or defiance, or if their cherished defenses have been breached, the narcissist may become hostile, intimidating, or even violent. This is done as much to punish their partner as it is to cause them anxiety and dread so that they will do what the narcissist desires.

Slander. In certain instances, along with the abuse, the narcissist will also launch a smear campaign against their partner. By reaching out to others, typically close friends and family, they hope to persuade them that something is wrong with their companion and that they are to blame for any issues.

Methodical Targeting. This is a fairly common tactic used in conjunction with abuse, word games, and other forms of assault. The narcissist systematically searches out the victim's real or perceived flaws and insecurities, which he or she then exploits. This is done to undermine their sense of self-worth and keep them off balance and unable to respond.

Pure Deceit. Normal individuals tend to tell the truth most of the time, but narcissists have no problem with lying when it serves their purposes. They will deceive by fabricating information, omitting pertinent details, or being evasive about their claims. While it is likely that the narcissist believes the lies, they also tell them to gain an advantage over their partner or other people with whom they are involved, to protect themselves, or to hide up something.

Exuding Negativity. This is another diversionary strategy. When a narcissist behaves in this manner, they are projecting any negative thoughts, emotions, or actions they may have had or are having onto their partner. This is closely related to Creating Guilt.

Shifting Standards. This is another tactic employed by the narcissist to maintain control over the victim (see below). By "moving the goalposts" in this manner, the narcissist endeavors to confuse and humiliate their victim, frequently to the point of inducing depression, apathy, and other psychological issues in the victim.

Harsh Judgement. When listening to the narcissist's anecdotes about other people, including their past relationships, the narcissist's partner heard harsh criticism of those individuals. They were likely moved to pity by the story at the time, oblivious that this aspect of the narcissist's character would one day be directed at them. This is one of the most prevalent ways in which narcissists make their victims feel inadequate, as it is consistent with their sense of superiority. They continually complain about what they perceive to be the victim's flaws, implying that they are subpar and could be better if they tried.

These are among the most common methods narcissists use to get under their victim's skin, but there are two others that deserve a bit more explanation. The use of gaslighting and the flying monkey.

Be wary of the Flying Monkey.

Someone who is a narcissist does not necessarily have to act alone. Christine Hammond, MS, LMHC dubbed them "Flying Monkeys" after the creatures sent by the Wicked Witch to capture Dorothy. They obey without inquiry and carry out her orders.

It works the same way with sociopaths and psychopaths, and even more so with narcissists. In any case, by delegating the dirty labor to a devoted subordinate, they can at least appear to have clean hands.

You have witnessed this in action, even if you are unaware. How many times have you witnessed a spokesperson for a narcissistic entertainer, politician, or CEO defending their employer after a scandal? What was Michael Cohen doing when he helped Donald Trump cover up his affair with Stormy Daniels? All of these are instances of flying primates.

Given the frequent public floggings they risk by obeying their narcissist's orders or covering up their actions, the question is why they do it. Because there are benefits for both parties, at least temporarily. According to Hammond, these flying primates frequently have their own psychological disorder, which enables them to mutually benefit from their relationship. The list comprises:

Disorder of Narcissistic Personality. So long as they are able to acquire power, influence, money, prestige, or some other advantage, the partnership will be successful. Once these benefits are lost or a greater benefit is presented, the narcissistic flying monkey departs and may even turn against their former idol.

Cohen is an excellent example of this because he betrayed Trump when it was to his advantage to do so.

Generalized Anxiety Disorder. In this instance, the flying monkey's persistent anxiety is attracted to the narcissist's arrogance, but only until the monkey's anxiety subsides.

Co-dependents. Codependency is fueled by the narcissist's need to be served and admired. The narcissist draws off the co-dependent's desire for purpose and fulfillment through caring for others. Once the co-dependent recovers and abandons their people-pleasing ways, the disappointed narcissist will, of course, depart.

Addicts. If the narcissist is the one supporting the addiction, the addict will slavishly do or say whatever will keep them in good standing with their supplier, just as a drug dealer can coerce their addicted clientele to do anything for the next dose. This relationship terminates in one of two ways: either the addict recovers and no longer requires what the narcissist provides, or the addiction worsens and the narcissist cuts them off because they become too dependent.

Dependent Personality Disorder. This dependent makes the narcissist feel so superior because, in addition to their obedience, they either include the narcissist in every decision they make or leave the decision to the narcissist alone. These connections rarely, if ever, terminate.

Sociopaths. In this case, the narcissist is useful to the sociopath, who will use the narcissist's outrageous behavior to conceal their own evil deeds, orchestrating everything while enabling the narcissist to believe they are in control. When circumstances change, these relationships tend to end, and it is to the sociopath's advantage to get clear of the narcissist.

The Functions of Rage

Anger. It can manifest naturally when the narcissist is disappointed, similar to a child's temper tantrum, but it typically manifests when the victim claps back at them and either threatens to expose the terrified child at their core or, worse, does expose it. It can also be used as a meticulously orchestrated tactic to coerce victims into submission.

Concerning anger, there are two distinct categories of narcissists to consider. The Grandiose narcissist, with his or her inflated ego and sense of entitlement, and the Vulnerable narcissist, who is concealing their deficiencies.

You Cannot Always Get What You Want, But You Always Get What You Need.

Typically, when we are dissatisfied with something, we either deal with the problem (Problem-focused Coping) or our emotions (Emotion-focused Coping). In any case, we deal with the disappointment, place it in context, and move on. However, this is not always how narcissists react.

It would be simple to assert that the typical reaction of a malignant narcissist is rage, particularly toward those they believe have managed to thwart their plans. It is an emotion-focused coping mechanism that may temporarily make the narcissist feel better, but it doesn't solve anything, and it alienates those who must interact with the narcissist and who may actually be able to help the situation. However, it is a bit more complicated than that. Studies indicate that ostentatious narcissists and vulnerable narcissists react differently to disappointment.

The grandiose variety of narcissists, with their inflated egos and elevated self-esteem, acclimate better to disappointment than vulnerable narcissists, who devote so much energy to concealing their inferiority complexes and low self-esteem.

Self-Awareness

The beginning of a romantic relationship with a narcissist is ideal. It appears to be taken from a storybook about genuine love, and with good reason; both the storybook and the narcissist's persona are fictional. The narcissist exerts great effort to attract his target, hoping to cause the target to fall hard and quickly for him. This is achieved through the use of mirroring and love bombardment.

The narcissistic romantic partner may send daily flowers and love notes to the target's workplace, in addition to continuously texting them about how beautiful they are and how perfect they are with them. Even if the target is uncomfortable, the romantic partner may invite the target out on numerous dates and press for the relationship to progress at a much faster rate than is typical. The narcissist will be more controlling than the target prefers, but the target will rationalize this behavior as excessively protective or trauma-related.

As the target grows more attached to the narcissist over time, the narcissist's façade begins to disintegrate. In the end, the mask disintegrates, revealing the narcissist in all his splendor, unmasked and intolerable, while you are too infatuated with the mask to leave its fragments on the floor without salvaging them. The narcissist is free to be himself when the victim is firmly attached to him. If he feels disrespected in any way, he may lash out at the target by saying hurtful or degrading things, or even by shouting and intimidating the target into submission.

In a narcissistic relationship, it is common to feel lonely or unimportant, as the narcissist ceases to prioritize your needs once he believes he has you securely in his grasp. As a result of the intensely amazing honeymoon period, he no longer needs to make the effort to win you over because you are already head-over-heels in love. He may employ other strategies, such as degrading or gaslighting, to keep you around. You will be left with a self-esteem as damaged as the narcissist's, but unlike the narcissist, yours can recover if you provide yourself with the necessary self-care.

At the conclusion of the relationship, the narcissist discards you; he may have moved on to a new source to satisfy his narcissistic supply, or he may have determined that maintaining you as useful is no longer worth the effort.

Can A Narcissist Possibly

Family Variation?

The point about narcissism is that every person on earth possesses narcissistic characteristics. We are all self-centered in our own ways, and we all desire to feel unique and to be the center of attention (under certain circumstances). Essentially, we are all attempting to distinguish ourselves and create an impact on the world. Therefore, narcissism is NOT a mental disorder. It only becomes a disorder when our narcissistic personality permeates every aspect of our existence. Only when we lack the ability to regulate our emotions and empathy does narcissism manifest as a personality disorder. In this light, narcissism is comparable to a personality disorder, such as borderline personality disorder, or a mood disorder, such as anxiety and melancholy. Can these be controlled, assisted, cured, or even altered? Yes, but it takes a great deal of effort, dedication, patience, and motivation to truly want to follow the advice of professionals in order to get better and manage narcissistic traits. To manage and cope with depression, you must alter various aspects of your life, such as your diet, the way you think, the way you worry, and the way you conduct your life in general. As with any mental or physical health issue, prescription medication will only mask the problem; in order to live a truly satisfying existence, you must put in the effort to overcome it.

To truly transform, narcissists must be comfortable with gaining a deeper emotional understanding of themselves in order to uncover their underlying shame and insecurities. They must learn how to make internal sacrifices, such as giving up the spotlight, being more conscious of their actions so they can place others first, and asking for assistance when they feel too ashamed to do so. To get a narcissist to want to change, they must be confronted with three factors:

For the narcissist to seek therapy or even contemplate therapy, there must be some leverage. This could include the fear of losing a loved one, the threat of losing their position or power, or the threat to their social status and reputation.

A therapeutic method

Similarly to how cognitive behavioral therapy (CBT) may be effective for anxiety sufferers and dialectical behavior therapy (DBT) may be effective for those with borderline personality disorder, narcissists must find an effective corrective therapy. A therapy such as schema therapy may be effective for narcissists because it examines the emotional narrative in the brain and concentrates below the intellectual level.

A skilled clinician

A competent therapist is someone who is neither easily attached nor easily persuaded. The ideal therapist for a narcissist is one who can set strong boundaries and does not provoke the narcissist. This would involve the therapist adopting a 'parenting' mentality towards the vulnerable part of the narcissist's psyche, while also holding them accountable for their thoughts and actions. When the 'perfect' psychologist is discovered, the narcissist will be taught how to transform. The modification will appear as follows:

Instructing them on how to comprehend their actions and how those actions produce negative emotions and thoughts (or vice versa).

Teaching the narcissist the consequences of what can occur as a result of these uncontrollable thoughts and emotions, which will result in them taking responsibility for ALL of their actions.

Permitting the narcissist to believe that he or she has options, and that based on those options, the narcissist determines the outcome (addressing the abusive behavior).

In the midst of anger, sadness, loneliness, etc., is able to teach the narcissist to recognize their choices as to why they are unhappy, as well as how to make different choices apart from how they feel.

As you can see, assisting a narcissist to transform can be a significant undertaking. However, if a narcissist is in denial about the existence of a problem, they will be unable to acknowledge their faults and would prefer to continue on their current path. The issue with this is that it can be risky to debate and fight with a narcissist, as it can be extremely difficult for the person who suffers because they do not comprehend why they do what they do. If you tell them directly that they are narcissists, their extreme sensitivity to criticism may harm you more than it harms their ego (How to Deal with a Narcissist, 2018).

A Genepool of Narcissists

When we discuss narcissism in the family, we are not referring to a single narcissist. Narcissistic tendencies or characteristics can affect the entire family, because narcissistic parents will inevitably produce narcissistic children. If you have a narcissistic child, someone in the family is likely to make justifications for him or her, which only makes the child more prone to maintaining their traits.

This can have a significant impact on every holiday spent with family, turning an afternoon with them into a memorable disaster.

This is what I mean when I state that narcissism impacts the entire family.

The Enabler: This includes a narcissist's spouse, the grandmother of a narcissistic child, or a close sibling.

In order to prevent further conflict, the enabler justifies the narcissist's actions.

The Flying Monkey: These family members can be anyone and are typically characterized as those who abuse other family members on the narcissist's behalf. For instance, an adult sister may have severed ties with a narcissistic sibling, and if the parent is the flying monkey, the sister may experience shame and guilt for having done so.

The Scapegoat: This family member has the courage to label the narcissist what they are: an individual with NPD. In lieu of lavishing the narcissist with acclaim and attention, they would rather tell it like it is. Due to their lack of support for the narcissist, the remainder of the family is typically upset with the scapegoat when this type of behavior occurs.

The Golden offspring is typically the offspring of a narcissistic parent who receives more praise and attention than other children. This creates conflict with other family members because the golden child can be used as a scapegoat or to manipulate other family members.

Often, the position of the golden child shifts when the child disagrees with or rejects their parent's idealized view, as the parent then becomes abusive and gaslights their own child (How to Deal with a Narcissist, 2018).

These family traits can make for chaotic holidays, and it may take time for the family as a unit to alter them. Although it is difficult for a single narcissist to change, in order to get the entire family on board and willing to change, certain therapeutic properties and a plan for how things will unfold are required. In addition, it must function for everyone;

otherwise, the entire project could fail and narcissistic traits could worsen.

Narcissistic Vacations

On family holidays, there are two possible outcomes: either the narcissist does not attend or they do and the gathering becomes contentious. Holidays such as Christmas, birthdays, Thanksgiving, New Year's, etc., can provoke the rage and perfectionist tantrums of narcissists. Attempting to enjoy the holidays involves and affects not only the narcissist but also the victim, particularly when the narcissist has succeeded in isolating the victim. If you have recently ended a relationship or ceased communicating with a narcissist, you may feel a void during the holidays, particularly if your personality revolved around them, e.g., doing things for them to avoid their wrath, engaging in guilt trips, and playing blame games.

Perhaps the most difficult aspect of moving on with your life is figuring out who you are now that you are no longer required to make continuous sacrifices and serve your narcissist.

However, holidays are ideal for getting back on track (if the narcissist is absent). They allow you to reopen up to your family, consume healthily, and reestablish relationships with formerly abundant supportive, positive people. In addition to rebuilding relationships, be sure to take care of yourself during the upcoming holidays. Consider your care in terms of how you would tend to your offspring, regardless of their emotional state. Exercise, get adequate rest, consume plenty of water, show yourself affection, tell yourself uplifting, confidence-building statements, etc. There are additional things you can do during the holiday season to recover from a narcissistic injury, including:

1. Be tolerant of yourself

You cannot expect to move on immediately, nor can you expect to feel joyful immediately. You may feel relieved until your memories of them remind you of the holiday pleasure you shared with them. Do what makes you joyful while keeping in mind that nothing has to be perfect and nothing has to be a complete failure. If you do not feel like participating in the festivities this year, give yourself more time because you do not have to do anything you do not want to.

2. Accept what was lost so that you can recreate it What traditions did you observe before the narcissist entered your life? Was it observing the holiday lights? Was it donning a costume for Halloween? Was it expressing gratitude by assisting someone in need? Whatever they were, you should keep doing them

because the narcissist has not harmed these 63 activities.

yet. If you do not pursue your former interests, you are solely responsible for their demise.

3. Recognize and avoid toxic individuals
Familiarize yourself with toxic individuals and those who are unsupportive of your endeavors, as their presence will hinder your recovery. Determine which of your acquaintances, family members, and relationships are here for you and which are not. Who wants the best for you and who only uses you to achieve their own ends. The toxic people in your life should be avoided (if possible), while the non-toxic individuals should be sought out for increased interaction.

4. Give, give, give

It is a proved fact that when we give to others, the 'feel-good' endorphin hormones in our brains are released. You can feel good about yourself while giving to others by donating, assisting someone with unloading their shopping, or simply giving them advice. Other ideas include removing litter from the roadways, planting trees, and volunteering at an animal or human shelter.

Because they are so familiar, it can be difficult to appreciate the holidays when the narcissist is absent. As soon as you begin practicing self-awareness and self-love, the days ahead will improve, and you will eventually chuckle at yourself for holding your breath for the abuser. Enjoy the absence of their additional burdens and tension, and remember to be kind to yourself and others.

Narcissists adore holidays, especially because it is simpler for them to take the spotlight and flaunt their superiority or perfection. They enjoy control, conflict, and the spotlight. What better method is there to be boastful and proud during the holidays? I have discussed how holidays can continue without the narcissist, but what if the narcissist is present? Here is what a holiday may look like when narcissists are present at family gatherings.

The curator's handiwork

Holidays provide the narcissist with an opportunity to display their superiority and contend with those around them, from the perfectly decorated Christmas tree to the best New Year's Eve fireworks. If you are invited, they are in charge of everything, but if you are not, don't feel left out because they will post about their success on social media and text you.

The abuse of gift-giving

As narcissists enjoy playing games and having power excursions, they are able to do both during the holidays. During a Christmas event where gifts are exchanged, for instance, the narcissist will not only flaunt their gifts but also inform others that their gifts are superior or will be superior. If you receive a gift from a narcissist, instead of being able to appreciate it, you will be forced to endure the enormous amount of effort they had to endure in order to obtain it for you. They will somehow make the gift-giving situation about how they should be thanked for the effort they put into acquiring the item they believed reminded them of you. The narcissist's gift-giving is focused solely on themselves.

The need for management

Have you ever witnessed or participated in the favoritism of one child over another, or if there are no siblings, one individual over everyone else? This is how a narcissist maintains control over a given situation. When they favor one individual but single out another, they invite criticism. This causes conflict because, in many cases, you are truly at the narcissist's residence, so the response is typically "if you don't like it, get out."

The self-centered mother (or father)

There is always a "scapegoat" in the family, as you learned earlier in this chapter. This is not necessarily limited to holiday gatherings. In essence, the person who speaks the truth.

However, this scapegoat consistently receives the most difficulty or abuse due to their characteristics. When they disagree with their narcissistic mother's version of the truth — a phenomenon known as gas lighting — all the other children rush to her defense in an attempt to avoid being abused or demeaned. The scapegoat, however, becomes the "black sheep" and is singled out by the mother and the rest of the family as a result of the scapegoat's critical behavior. While the scapegoat is ostracized or singled out, everyone else views and interprets events in the same manner as their mother because this is how they were reared.

This is the discarding phase of narcissistic abuse.

While holidays are intended to be enjoyable, they are almost always marred when a narcissist hosts or attends. The best way to cope with a holiday involving narcissistic people is to enjoy the event, tolerate the individual, and then avoid them for as long as possible while making better decisions and building your own life. However, can a narcissistic family transform? As you now know, the answer is yes, but it requires a great deal of effort and labor. To overcome the influence of narcissism, the cycle must be broken.

Start the Healing Process and Regain Your Confidence and Self-Esteem

It takes time to recover from the violence inflicted by a narcissistic partner. It is one of the most overused cliches, but for good reason: time is the greatest curative.

Not to minimize the psychological injury caused by physical abuse, but emotional abuse is arguably worse. It's harm that is mostly invisible to others, and some of it will be invisible to you, at least for the time being. It is detrimental to your psyche and all aspects of your personality, from your courage to your sense of self-worth and well beyond.

Similar to lacerating a wound, you will need to carefully locate and extract the poison from its hiding place. Complete recovery from emotional abuse can take months or even years, so your first objective must be to acknowledge that you have a long road ahead of you.

However, you can rest assured that this journey will contain a little piece of splendor. Many victims of abuse characterize their recovery positively as a period of awakening and self-discovery on an unprecedented scale.

Even though every abusive relationship is unique, a common thread is that the abuser gradually erodes the victim's character. Your abuser deemed you too outgoing, too independent, too social, or too flirtatious, so they made the necessary steps to change you. In the meantime, you spent the duration of your relationship conforming to your abuser's whims; they likely dictated how you spent your time, who you spent time with, what you ate, and how you dressed.

At the time, and perhaps even now, you were unaware that it was occurring. It occurs incrementally, step by step, making it difficult to see the big picture and recognize how much you have changed.

You will have the opportunity to recover these lost aspects of your personality during your recuperation. At some point, you will realize that YOU determine what you do this weekend, what you consume for dinner, and whether or not you pursue a new career. If the relationship lasted a long time, you may have entirely forgotten what that is; you may have even changed naturally over time, outside of your abuser's influence, and now have the opportunity to explore new interests and desires.

Don't despair, even though it will be a difficult journey and you will continue to discover holes in the dam for a long time. The outcome of this healing could be the greatest thing that has ever happened to you, or at the very least an enormously positive step in the right direction.

The Broken Elements

Understanding is essential to any endeavor, so let's examine the harm this abuse has caused you – the harm you will labor to repair. Again, your situation will be unique, so it will be your responsibility to determine which of these apply and to what extent. Due to the fact that we are dealing with concealed abuse, it may take time for some of them to surface.

Sense of Self

Let's begin with the most obvious: your sense of self. Your abuser employed manipulation, recriminations, and any other means necessary to subjugate you. Over time, your identity began to transfer to your abuser, and you began to unconsciously rely on them to determine who you were and what you desired. It was probably easier that way; your subconscious mind probably took precautions to shield you from further unease and discomfort. Somewhere along the line, your sense of self was compromised to the extent that you no longer know how to make decisions that are in your own best interests, and you are unsure of who or what you are without your abuser to tell you.

The Desire for Affection

Abusers use affection as a compensation, similar to how dog owners use treats to train their pets. The "love" you received was, to say the least, conditional, and you only received it if you satisfied your abuser.

Now that even this meager taste of affection has been eliminated from your life, the repercussions may be even more profound. You are conditioned to do whatever it takes to receive affection, yet you still crave someone who will listen to you, comprehend you, love you, and respect you.

Be wary of this type of harm, as it can sometimes propel you directly into the embrace of another abuser. Until you have a grasp on it, it is usually best to avoid romantic relationships and be cautious about other relationships. Narcissistic abuse is not limited to romantic relationships, and the neediness you are currently experiencing is like blood in the water to an abuser.

Psychological Independence

It is unlikely that your abuser physically confined you, but they did construct an emotional cage around you. By criticizing, complaining, gaslighting, and shunning you when you misbehaved, they restricted what you could and could not do and say. You, in turn, internalized these limitations and came to believe that your life must be lived within them; breaking them was inconceivable and still causes you anxiety.

In the aftermath of the relationship, you will observe that you are affected in a variety of ways. You may place too much emphasis on what others think of you, thereby transferring the responsibility for your actions that your oppressor assumed to someone else rather than to yourself. You might fear new experiences and/or change. You may resist assuming responsibility for things, regardless of their apparent insignificance. Breaking that cage will take time; you may have gotten rid of your abuser, but the cage is still there, even if it is no longer entirely intact.

Fear of Errors

When you made what they deemed to be a blunder, your abuser punished you in unusual and cruel ways. You were shamed for your poor behavior, criticized for exceeding your boundaries, or your abuser withheld affection until you made amends.

Shame and embarrassment are natural responses when we make a mistake; they are nature's method of preventing us from repeating the error. These emotions are a normal part of existence, and most of the time we can accept that. No one enjoys the sensation, but we learn the necessary lessons and move on.

In your case, however, humiliation and embarrassment have been used as weapons against you, and their effects have been amplified to the point where they no longer teach you to avoid certain behaviors in the future, but rather to obey.

You have developed an unhealthy aversion to these emotions over time, to the point where you would likely do almost anything to avoid them. But while avoiding shame and embarrassment is precisely why they exist, emotional abuse crosses the line to the point where you no longer want to take any "risk" or attempt new things out of fear of the outcome.

Concern for the Future

Existence of dread in your life is associated with avoiding shame and embarrassment. You were punished for any aberrant behavior you may have displayed while you were trapped in that abusive relationship.

Perhaps your abuser verbally abused you for an hour at the time you told your companions you would be spending the evening with them. Perhaps they took one look at the sexy ensemble you purchased and remarked that you appeared ridiculous. Perhaps you were met with resistance when you suggested a weekend getaway.

You learned from these responses that you should not make any new decisions; the future belonged to your abuser, not you. You have been left in a mental state in which you dread making decisions that will affect your future, despite the fact that your abuser is no longer present to punish you or make those decisions for you.

This dread can be precisely what keeps a victim in an abusive relationship – even the decision to leave can be an insurmountable obstacle. You have already overcome that particular obstacle, but if you permit it, anxiety may still hinder your recovery.

Disconnection from the World

Emotional abusers have a propensity for isolating their victims from the outside world, assuming complete control of their lives and decisions, and isolating other loved ones who may wield uncontrollable influence. Despite being removed from the situation, you may continue to feel entirely cut off from the rest of the world and uncertain of your place in it.

Some victims feel numb, as their hearts have become so closed and guarded that they cannot feel either pleasure or pain. You feel hopeless and as though you have no true future – you're too damaged, there's no way to return to normalcy.

Typically, this occurs when the emotional impact of terminating the relationship would be too great to handle all at once. Your mind is capable of protecting you in ways you did not anticipate and possibly are unaware of. This detachment is in no way detrimental to your healing, as it enables you to cope with the aftermath one step at a time.

Anger and Resentment

Why did you experience this? What have you ever done to merit such a horrible treatment? How could someone believe it was acceptable to behave in such a manner toward someone they professed to care about? These are typical concerns that victims ask themselves, and the resentment, anger, and frustration that accompany them are completely normal.

This particular aspect of the fallout is something that can gain strength over time and have physical effects, such as altered blood pressure, a racing pulse, and an inability to sleep. It is something you must let go of, but you should also be grateful for your anger. The fact that you are furious that this happened to you demonstrates that you recognize it was not something you deserved or were destined to experience.

Be cautious, however, as some victims may channel their anger inwards. How could you have allowed this to occur? Why did you not anticipate this? Often, the shame of being a victim prevents us from obtaining the assistance we require or admitting to others that all is not well. Meanwhile, we torment ourselves with "what if" scenarios, condemning ourselves for our victimization rather than our abuser for manipulating our good intentions. Among the most challenging aspects of being the victim of an offender is letting go of the self-blame that plagues you in the aftermath.

Evaluation of Oneself and Others

Similarly, this one may not appear at the start of your recovery. Nonetheless, it can become obsessive over time. You may find yourself excessively analyzing everything you do and everything others around you do, establishing impossible standards for how you behave and how others treat you.

Your comprehension of "good behavior" in yourself and others has been put to the test; you may no longer know precisely what to anticipate. You do not know how to trust others, any of whom could abuse you in the same manner your abuser did, and you do not know how to behave yourself.

As you become reintegrated into the world and begin to socialize once more, this, too, will balance off over time. If you are able to forgive yourself for what you perceive to be past errors, you will eventually be able to release this judgment. You will gain the ability to trust others as you relearn what you once knew about determining the intentions of others.

Emotional Distress

It's tough to leave an abusive relationship completely intact in terms of your mental and emotional health. Depression, anxiety, and even PTSD and suicidal ideation are prevalent among victims of this type of maltreatment. Your emotions have been unshackled from the tight grasp of your abuser and will inevitably be all over the place for a while as you slowly settle back into your equilibrium.

If you are having trouble sleeping or staying asleep, if you feel lonely and helpless, if you have used or are considering using alcohol or drugs to ease the pain, if you have withdrawn from the world and your loved ones, if you feel anxious or are having panic attacks, if you are experiencing sudden outbursts of anger or are having flashbacks, you may be experiencing a severe emotional reaction that requires professional intervention.

There is no shame in seeking help – please, please consider doing so. Find a counselor or psychologist and let them assist you over this hurdle, as it's not one you should contemplate alone.

Your Point of Origin

You may immediately recognize one or more of them as applicable to your current situation; you may suspect that others are occurring but be uncertain; and you may believe that others are imminent. Again, your circumstance is unique, and there is no standard formula for the effects of an abusive relationship.

But it is possible to determine the type of survivor you have become – how the symptoms combined during the relationship and how they are now affecting you. You may fit into multiple categories, but you will likely identify most strongly with one.

Understanding how emotional abuse has affected you is crucial not only for your road to recovery. It will help you identify the obstacles you must overcome to restore your emotional health, but it will also assist you in avoiding a repeat of this suffering in the future.

The "symptoms" of emotional abuse manifest long before we make the difficult decision to leave the abusive relationship. They are created during the abuse and develop into a pattern that would almost certainly be repeated if you were to encounter another abuser.

Do not neglect that there may already be another abuser in your life, such as a parent, a friend, a coworker, or a boss. Abusive behavior can be exhibited by nearly anyone. Even if you have been a victim in the past, this does not imply that you must continue to be victimized by this individual.

You have likely also heard the old cliche about individuals who always choose the "wrong type" in their romantic relationships. This is a distinct possibility when it comes to abuse; for example, consider the symptom of loss of self. You lost the ability to make decisions about yourself and your future as a result of your abuser; it seems only natural, if you are not fully healed from the experience, that you would seek a new companion who can make up for this lack, plunging you back into the abusive pattern.

Chapter 5: Methods for Handling a Narcissistic Mother

Yes, it could be difficult for a child to grow up with a narcissistic parent, especially a mother.

You have arrived at the correct destination. This article describes how to recognize narcissistic motherly behavior and how to effectively cope with it. This article contains advice and suggestions for avoiding narcissistic parents.

What is the definition of a narcissistic mother?

In psychology, narcissism is defined as "selfishness characterized by a sense of entitlement, a lack of empathy, and a desire for admiration" In common parlance, narcissism signifies "excessive interest in or adoration of one's physical appearance and self"

When vanity, self-love, and ego exceed a tolerable level, they transform into something negative. This is frequently referred to as narcissism. Like the severity of most diseases, it can vary considerably. And its effect is proportional to the severity of the condition.

You may have observed narcissistic behavior in your mother, but you should not immediately conclude that she is an extreme narcissist. People with narcissistic tendencies can fall anywhere on the narcissistic spectrum, from a true narcissist with narcissistic personality disorder (NPD) to someone exhibiting a milder variant of narcissistic symptoms.

A typical characteristic of a narcissistic mother is a sense of entitlement or self-importance. She lacks empathy, demands others' admiration, and cannot tolerate criticism. She considers herself superior to others and expects special treatment. To achieve her goals, she will gleefully bring others down and exploit her offspring. The worst trait of a narcissist is that they are oblivious to the destruction they perpetrate on others.

A narcissistic mother will manipulate her children to make her life easier and more enjoyable. Instead of fulfilling her motherly duties, she would blatantly exploit them for her own purposes. She is least concerned about the well-being of her offspring.

All of this neglect and exploitation will result in the offspring of narcissistic mothers feeling unloved, invalidated, bewildered, and lacking in self-esteem.

Phrases used by narcissistic mothers

"You are so ungrateful."

"I told you so."

"You've made the bed, so now sleep in it."

"You are creating too much out of nothing."

"You are too emotionally sensitive for your own good."

"I'm simply trying to help."

"I'm saying this for your own good."

"Is there anything wrong with you?"

You will feel regret upon my departure.

"You think you are so smart."

How could you speak to me in such a manner?

"You just care for yourself."

"I'm the only one who will ever care about you."

"I have sacrificed my entire life for you."

"I have no idea what you're referring to."

Manifestations of a narcissist mother

As previously stated, not all mothers who exhibit narcissistic behavior have NPD. However, there is no doubt that narcissistic behavior of any degree can have a devastating effect on the fragile minds of young children. The repercussions of their selfish tendencies can be detrimental and harmful to the child.

Consider the following indicators of narcissism in your mother.

Her interactions are always centered on herself.

You and your accomplishment are lauded to others, but you are not recognized for it.

When you are harmed as a result of her actions, she places the responsibility on others.

Is constantly beaming and sweet-talking in the presence of others, but vicious, harsh, and authoritarian when alone.

You are shamed for not immediately complying with her requests.

She takes you on a guilt trip by listing the favors she's performed for you.

She is willing to be venomous and vindictive to achieve her goals.

She is superior to chameleons in her ability to change colors rapidly and effortlessly.

She is harsh and controlling at home, but her performance in front of those she deems significant will earn her an Oscar.

She causes you to experience anxiety and dread and can lower your confidence and self-esteem.

Dealing with a mother who is egocentric

If you believe you have a narcissistic mother based on the aforementioned signs, here are some tips and suggestions to help you deal with her. Be forewarned that interacting with narcissistic parents is not easy. However, inaction is also not an option because it could be destructive.

1. Stay cool

Emotional responses to her narcissistic behavior may exacerbate the situation. Frequently, they say things to elicit a response from you and then use it to further their objective. Don't be fooled by this. Stay tranquil.

2. Plan your responses

She is so cunning and cunning that it is impossible to catch up to her. She always gets you exactly where she wants you to be. To avoid this, you can plan your responses to her stimuli in advance. Obviously, she will go further and create new ones. To keep up with her in this, you must remain constantly vigilant.

3. Set constraints

This may help with some narcissistic mothers, but in most cases it will not. She will disregard your boundaries and traipse all over you. Despite the high likelihood of failure, you should try this and see if it works.

4. Learn to surrender

You are not responsible for narcissistic conduct. Typically, it is neither your nor your mother's fault, as she has a personality disorder. Accept the facts and avoid taking her words, behavior, and actions personally. Nothing she says about you is accurate. It is merely her afflicted psyche speaking.

5. Maintain some distance

A narcissistic mother will prey on anyone she can capture. Therefore, avoid her as much as possible. This may be difficult if you are young and dependent on her. Use your intelligence to devise creative solutions to avoid her.

Take measures to improve your mood.

When one's confidence and self-esteem are low, the words and actions of a narcissistic mother can be very damaging. Work on them and implement measures to raise them to normal levels. This will ensure that the wounds are less severe and excruciating. You may also engage in activities or other diversions to avoid studying this topic.

Obtain assistance

You may not be able to handle this on your own, especially if the condition is severe. You may seek advice from a reliable individual regarding how to deal with your narcissistic mother. Friends, instructors, other family members, and colleagues are the appropriate contacts in this situation.

Reading about and gaining a deeper understanding of this mental state may assist you in choosing the appropriate response to the situation at hand. A competent therapist may also be helpful.

The In-Law's Narcissistic Mother

Have you recently married and discovered that your mother-in-law is extremely difficult to bear? Or, have you been married for a long time and always had a difficult relationship with your husband's mother?

Individuals' relationships with their spouse's family members are undoubtedly always going to be the most difficult. Especially if she is narcissistic, a mother-in-law can be challenging to get along with. Developing a healthy relationship with narcissistic parents is always challenging, but the mother-in-law dynamic can make it especially so.

This article focuses on how to make future interactions with a narcissistic mother-in-law as straightforward as feasible. Several of the strategies we describe can also be employed to cope with narcissistic parents.

Indicators Of A Narcissistic In-Law Mother

First, however, we will examine the signs of a narcissistic mother-in-law. Many of these signs will be the same for all narcissistic parents, but they will frequently be amplified when coping with an in-law mother. This is because of the mother-son relationship between her mother and her son, which becomes threatening when competitive.

1. excessively combative

A narcissist is frequently extremely competitive and always desires to triumph, regardless of the circumstances. Even in the most straightforward disagreements or discussions, a person with narcissistic personality disorder will always want to ensure that their viewpoint prevails. When it comes to any physical activity, the narcissist will always seek victory. This may be difficult to tolerate, but rest assured that many individuals struggle with being too competitive in relationships.

2. Never volunteering to assist

Perhaps one of the most challenging aspects of dealing with a narcissistic mother-in-law, as well as a significant indicator that she is a narcissist, is that she never offers assistance. This is a characteristic of this type of personality disorder because the individual is too self-absorbed to realize that others may require assistance. Sadly, it may be the case that they never offered to help with even the smallest chores around the house if they are living with you, nor did they offer to assist with larger duties such as caring for children or supporting you during a difficult time.

Always putting down family relations

As a result of their extremely competitive nature, narcissists in a family will continuously put down other family members. This could very well include you, and in reality, no one is ever immune to a narcissist's caustic remarks. This may be extremely difficult to recognize with in-laws because the interpersonal dynamic prevents us from informing them that their comments are detrimental. However, when it comes to in-laws who disparage other close relatives, keep in mind that every family has difficult relationships.

4. Repeating the same tale frequently

Another significant symptom of a narcissist is the individual's repetition of the same story. This is a characteristic of narcissistic behavior, particularly among in-laws, because it demonstrates a lack of self-awareness. They may be unaware that they have repeated a story to multiple individuals. Because you are more likely to see your relatives frequently, you are more likely to hear the same stories repeatedly. It can be quite exhausting, so consider ways to listen with only one ear.

5. Trying to control all circumstances

When it comes to narcissistic in-laws, the fact that they prefer to dominate all situations and feel in charge is a particularly difficult trait to manage. This may be extremely stressful for one's self-esteem because it may cause one to doubt their own abilities. However, despite their desire to appear in charge, they should recognize that this desire stems from a lack of self-confidence.

How to Manage a Narcissistic Mother-in-Law

Here, we examine ways you can assist yourself in preparing for interactions with your mother-in-law or other in-laws who may exhibit narcissistic traits.

1. Patience

Tolerating a person who is so self-absorbed as a narcissist may be the most difficult thing to do. It might appear too obvious and something you have already tried to address the issue. However, there is no danger in attempting to extend your tolerance with the person who raised the person you fell in love with. You may find that your relationship with your in-laws improves beyond measure if you combine patience with a few of the additional strategies listed below.

2. Create exit strategies

Obviously, it would be difficult to tolerate a person whose narcissistic behaviors cause them to be consistently negative. In any other circumstance, it is unlikely that you would make plans to see them again. It is impossible for this to occur with your in-laws. Therefore, to cope with situations that you find unpleasant, you should discuss with your partner a method for removing yourself from them before they become overwhelming. This may imply that you can have a signal indicating that you must depart because you have had enough. Or it could be a plan to leave at a specific time so that you know you have something to strive for.

3. Inquire about their lives

It may seem counterintuitive to ask a narcissist about themselves, but doing so can be a useful tool for dealing with their difficult idiosyncrasies. By asking them about themselves, you assume control of the situation and steer the conversation in the desired direction. In addition, narcissists enjoy talking about themselves and will be grateful to the person who gives them the opportunity to do so.

4. Request direct assistance

If one of your greatest grievances with the narcissist in your life is that they never offer assistance, simply ask them for assistance. Often, narcissists are too self-absorbed to recognize that you have problems and require assistance. Tell them precisely how they can help you, and you may be surprised by how anxious they are to provide you with the assistance you require.

5. Talk to your companion

Communicating with one's spouse may be the most obvious piece of advice that individuals overlook when dealing with a narcissistic mother-in-law. Because they know their mother so well and are likely keenly aware of their flaws, this may be a highly effective and substantial strategy for addressing this issue. In reality, they would concur with you on how disagreeable narcissistic behavior is. Sometimes it is sufficient to know that someone agrees with you.

Give them obligations

The best method to deal with a difficult and narcissistic mother-in-law is to assign them duties. This may significantly improve your relationship with them because it demonstrates your reliance and reverence for them. They enjoy feeling needed, desired, and cherished. Therefore, if they are aware that you require their assistance in some fashion, they may start focusing on the responsibilities you assign them rather than engaging in narcissistic behavior.

7. Display sympathy

Display empathy

Even though a person is a narcissist, this does not preclude them from occasionally experiencing emotional pain. In addition, it is often the case with personality disorders that a person's past has contributed to their behavior. If you demonstrate compassion and understanding for their past, you may find that you begin to develop a stronger connection with them, which could lead to a future improvement in your relationship.

8. Rely on their knowledge

As narcissists enjoy talking about themselves and are continuously looking for opportunities to do so, it may be advantageous to solicit their opinion on various topics. As previously discussed, they desire to feel essential or desired and are eager to share their experiences. Additionally, you may find it advantageous to see things from their perspective, which may make you feel more at ease with them.

9. Recognize them

When you rely on a person's experience and make an effort to be more sensitive to their past, you create a picture of them that you may not have noticed at first glance. When you have a greater understanding of the image, it may be useful to attempt to comprehend it even more than before. This knowledge can help you have much more patience with them when they inevitably exhibit the self-centered behavior you find so irritating.

When is your mother-in-law self-absorbed?

It might be difficult to deal with a narcissistic mother-in-law. This is a difficult relationship because you never want to place your partner in an uncomfortable situation. Try to be patient and recognize that there are other important relationships in your life.

How do I deal with a narcissistic in-law mother?

Dealing with a narcissistic mother-in-law can be difficult, but it is possible. You must develop your own method of coping and also address the underlying causes. Examine the preceding list for suggestions that could proactively strengthen your relationship with her.

Conclusion

When interacting with a narcissistic mother, you must be mindful of the "don'ts" even as you determine your response. Do not point out her mistakes, attempt to correct her, compare her to others, or demand that she apologize. Do not anticipate her to alter.

You must avoid self-criticism and self-injury. Realize that everything she says is based on her imagination and has nothing to do with you or the truth.

There are steps you can take to protect yourself and appreciate life despite the presence of an unsupportive parent if you are living with them.

Undoubtedly, a relationship with a narcissistic mother-in-law is extremely challenging. It can be arduous, depleting, and incredibly aggravating. Worse yet, you may not want to put your partner in the middle of any tensions between you and her, but it can be difficult not to, particularly when her self-centered behavior crosses the line.

Nevertheless, it is evident that this relationship will not last. As long as you are married to her offspring, your mother-in-law will remain in your existence. Therefore, it may be prudent to confront her behavior head-on and adopt a proactive stance towards it. Therefore, endeavoring to exhibit a little more tolerance and understanding with her can often go a long way. In addition, if you make them feel essential, you may find that your dynamic improves and her typical narcissistic traits irritate you less.

Chapter 6: Retrieve Your Life

It is time to learn how to reclaim your life after narcissistic abuse now that you have learned how to make amends with the people you care about, most crucially yourself. This can be challenging because, if you were raised in a narcissistic home, narcissistic traits are ingrained in your brain. Reclaiming your life requires more than just letting go of a narcissistic parent, grandparent, or sibling. It involves learning how to discharge the narcissist within you. Self-esteem, self-worth, self-trust, and self-love are the four pillars necessary to overcome the internal and external violence you have endured.

Self-esteem

Imagine having complete mental, physical, and behavioral control. There is no longer a third party influencing you to believe one thing and manipulating you to do another. Self-esteem involves being aware of your perception of the world and the impact you have on your surroundings. If you have consistently sabotaged everything around you to the extent of self-destruction, your self-esteem is low. Ultimately, high self-esteem would be evident if you are confident in who you are as an individual without bending to the desires or expectations of others.

Self-esteem is increased primarily through positive self-talk. If you continually listen to your inner critic enumerate the reasons why you cannot do something, you will eventually begin to believe it. You may attempt to escape this negative self-talk by spending money on unnecessary items or by experimenting with addictive substances such as alcohol and tobacco. This behavior indicates a lack of effort. While self-esteem is determined by how you carry yourself, your reputation may not be the greatest at this time. This can further diminish levels of self-esteem and contentment. Self-esteem also decreases when you try and attempt to accomplish something, such as mending your narcissistic relationship, but you keep failing no matter what you do or how hard you try.

To rebuild your self-esteem, you must do things you are excellent at (such as working or being creative) and acknowledge your weaknesses (such as forming a narcissistic relationship). Moreover, addressing both of these aspects increases fortitude. Whether you were reared in a narcissistic environment or met a narcissist who drew you into one, the reason your self-esteem may be low is because you took everything that happened to you personally. As you should have learned by now, narcissistic abuse should not be taken personally because they have successfully projected their burden and flaws onto you. When restoring your self-esteem, you should ask yourself, "What can I control right now?" Start taking better care of yourself; this is a variable you can always control. Consequently, you may have developed depression, anxiety, or the initial phases of PTSD. As a result, you may not have the desire to get out of bed, dress, take a shower, or consume. These are all straightforward tasks that you can begin managing immediately.

Your self-esteem journey may start off slowly. You will not regain it all at once, but gradually as you continue to do minor things every day that make you feel good and better about yourself. The greater your sense of accomplishment, the more confidence you will have to undertake larger tasks, such as outlining that creative story or creating the business plans you've been putting off for years. Remember to reward yourself for every accomplishment, regardless of size. This will teach your brain that you are moving in the correct direction, which will assist you in silencing your inner critic.

Self-worth

Self-esteem is, in a nutshell, the confidence to be who you are without regard for others' desires or expectations. Nonetheless, self-worth elevates self-esteem to a higher level. It is about knowing what you stand for, remaining true to your values, and having enough self-respect to defend everything that makes you who you are. Self-worth is ultimately about embracing yourself as you are and understanding what you're worth and what you deserve, which is to never again be abused by a narcissist.

If you experience an excessive amount of guilt, shame, embarrassment of yourself, and unworthiness, then you have low self-esteem. This would make sense if you'd been told your entire existence that you're not good enough or that you're only good enough when you accomplish extraordinary feats. You were instructed to be a perfectionist and to view failure as intolerable. However, this way of thinking diminishes your sense of self-worth because, if you are not "perfect," you are not deserving of what you desire. Probably, the narcissist made you feel like you didn't have a voice or that you weren't free to say and do as you pleased. Instead, you were taught that failure is frowned upon, that negative emotions are intolerable, and that your value was null and void if you were not living to serve them. A lifetime of this can cause you to second-guess and compromise all of your decisions when you eventually take a stand and decide to cut ties and strike out on your own. Low levels of self-esteem will keep you connected to the narcissist because they have implanted in your brain the belief that you will never achieve success in life without them.

Have you ever been described as a "pushover"? That you are overly empathetic or put the requirements of others ahead of your own to 'impress' or make yourself feel better? Lack of self-worth is when you find it difficult to stand up for yourself; it's when someone moves in front of you and you remain silent and receptive. It is when you convince yourself you are weak for being unable to say no. Then, when you do say no, you beat yourself up out of fear that the other person will be angry with you, which you cannot bear.

As long as you continue to feel incompetent and worthless, the narcissist will always have control over you. To develop and rebuild your self-worth, you must start focusing on your bravery and the things for which you are appreciative. These things can be as simple as being thankful for waking up another day or that you have learned difficult life lessons that have given you a new perspective. Many people do not understand what a narcissist is and are fortunate to escape if they recognize their abuser's signs and motivations. Be thankful that you are one person who has learned about them and is learning how to surmount the abuse. Developing courage entails taking risks to advance in one's existence. Every day, you must work towards your objectives and believe that you are as important as anyone else. Start by taking small risks, such as speaking up during a family gathering or telling someone to stand in the rear of the line. Apply for the position you desire or return to education. Taking risks involves identifying your anxieties and gradually overcoming them. When you do something wholeheartedly, you develop fortitude, which increases your confidence, self-respect, and sense of self-worth.

Identifying your values and adhering to them is a further method for enhancing your sense of self-worth. Create them and live by them so that they are not crossed and you are not harmed again. Protect yourself by guarding your morals and having the confidence to stand up for what you desire most in the world.

Self-trust

Ultimately, self-confidence is the ability to tune into your intuition (behind your inner-critic) and listen to that gut sensation that tells you to pursue something or to avoid it. Self-confidence involves believing in yourself and having faith that you know what's best for you.

Lack of self-confidence is rooted in feelings of self-doubt and dread. When you refrain from doing something or avoid something out of dread, you strengthen your self-doubt. Fear can either hold you back or propel you forward, but it generally encompasses everything. You may dread taking risks and forming relationships. You might be afraid of placing yourself out there or making choices. Do you feel like you continually second-guess your decisions? Perhaps you feel as though you know what to do, but due to a lack of self-confidence (and narcissistic abuse), you overthink your decisions to the point that you back out? For instance, someone cuts in front of you, and you feel the need to retaliate due to your low self-esteem. Then, as you attempt to speak, you freeze; a knot forms in your midsection, and you begin to second-guess your next move to the point where you simply remain silent. A lack of self-confidence can impede a person to the point where making decisions becomes a chore. These choices may include what to purchase at the grocery store, where to consume dinner, and what to wear to your best friend's birthday party.

As if your insecurities about most things weren't bad enough, your lack of self-confidence makes them worse. You can develop self-confidence by tuning into your intuition. When you listen to your intuition, you conduct frequent self-checks. How am I currently feeling? How does this person make me feel? What are my thoughts on this concept? Observe how these concepts are not based on second-guessing, but rather on tuning into your thoughts, feelings, and desires. When conducting a self-check, be sure to attend to your first or second response; otherwise, you will find yourself second-guessing and over-thinking, which will perpetuate self-trust issues. After achieving complete alignment with your instinctual nature, the next step is to act. For instance, if your body and mind indicate that the energy you receive from a particular person is off, you should proceed with caution. The more times your intuition proves correct, the more confidence you will develop in yourself.

Self-love

This act of reclaiming your life after narcissistic maltreatment is possibly the most crucial self-development skill you can acquire. Self-love involves nurturing one's inner child and providing for oneself in ways that no one else can. When you learn to accept yourself as you are, every other aspect (self-worth, self-trust, and self-esteem) naturally falls into position.

When you do not appreciate or care for yourself (your inner child), you may experience feelings of self-criticism and self-denial. These emotions are a result of the narcissistic abuse, as one of their techniques was to distort your perception of reality and sense of judgment. People-pleasing, always saying yes when you want to say no, and sacrificing your own needs for the sake of others are the behaviors that result. Do you continually criticize yourself? Feel you're not decent enough, worthy enough, or even intelligent enough? Do you uphold your personal obligations? Or make frequent unfulfilled promises because you reserve your free time for others. This is the experience of lacking self-love. Your behaviors or habits may include not eating when you are famished (or eating too much), not drinking enough water, smoking more than you should, drinking alcohol frequently, and never making time for yourself. You have too many tasks and not enough time to complete them. Or do you find yourself becoming anxious over trivial matters because you neglected to remember them? Self-love and care involve refraining from attempting the unattainable. Give yourself time to slow down and purchase that book you've been waiting for, watch that movie you've been longing to see, or soak in the tub for longer than usual.

One thing to realize about making concessions for others is that everything is significant in terms of your personal development. So perhaps your acquaintance invited you to the mall, but you had plans to take a bath, nap, or get your hair done. You instead say no to yourself and yes to them out of fear of disappointing them. It may not appear to be significant, but it is. When you compromise yourself, you jeopardize your integrity, health, mental serenity, sanity, and well-being. Lack of self-love can be extremely detrimental over time, even if these effects do not manifest immediately. So, what are some methods to rediscover self-love?

Identify the things in your world that you detest the most. Determine what you can alter and, if nothing, how you can change your perspective. If you are in a narcissistic relationship, for instance, you can alter this by leaving. If you detest where you live but are locked into a one-year lease, consider how you can change your perspective. How many months are left, and perhaps you need those months to save for something greater in the future? Is it your health that makes you unhappy? Commit to going to the gym and eating healthier foods. Work on self-acceptance if you are unable to alter your physical appearance because you are fixated on your freckles or the fact that you have brown eyes when you desire green. Self-acceptance is accompanied by self-approval and self-assurance. If this is the case, there may be an underlying cause of the issue. When we struggle to embrace our self-image, it is frequently because we have been told that our legs are too fat or that our eyes are too wide. Keep in mind that you are the only person who defines your self-image. Self-worth gives you the respect you need to overcome your lack of self-acceptance, which is exhibited by your confidence.

How to Frequently Say No

One of the primary issues for individuals who lack confidence and self-esteem is their inability to say no. As previously stated, their internal fears cause them to sacrifice their desires and requirements for the sake of others. You may believe that if you say no to people, they will lose respect for you and even vanish from your existence. Frequently, the opposite of this dread occurs. Not only will you develop a new sense of self-respect, but so will others, as confidence and self-esteem are highly attractive qualities. When others observe your efforts to improve yourself, they will respect your boundaries more and may even follow suit. However, those individuals who truly leave your life or become extremely angry with you for saying no will reveal why they were in your life in the first place. Typically, individuals who are overly sensitive to disappointment or rejection have internal issues, and this has nothing to do with you. In addition, reclaiming your life includes identifying these toxic individuals and avoiding them. Therefore, learning to say no is technically a gain for you regardless of your perspective.

Perhaps you have preconceived conceptions about saying no, such as being disliked, being afraid of rejection, or appearing careless or selfish. The crucial takeaway from this is that if you have these fears, you can cross narcissism off your list. Because narcissists do not have these concerns, the fact that you do speaks volumes about your character. Nevertheless, stating no is a crucial step towards developing self-confidence and self-esteem. It is a method for building on these so that you no longer fell for the narcissist's abusive tactics. Instead of immediately agreeing to a request for a favor, take a moment to consider the following steps before responding.

Keep your responses straightforward and simple: This procedure may make you feel impolite, but you are not required to be uncouth when you decline. Simply begin by considering your response, and if you wish to decline, say, "I'm sorry, but I already have plans for this afternoon, so I cannot assist you." Or, "I cannot commit to assisting you at this time because I have other obligations." These responses are concise, straightforward, and to the point.

If someone comes to you demanding an immediate response, you should never give in at that instant. Buy yourself some time by stating, "I apologize, but I need more time to consider this. I will contact you again." When you take extra time to consider your response, you will be more confident in saying no in the future.

Compromise: Only make a compromise if you genuinely want to assist but have limited time to do so. Let them know you have plans, but you will be available within xxx hours, and negotiate a time to assist them.

Refusal and rejection are distinct concepts: Refusal is the act of rejecting a request, whereas rejection is the act of rejecting a person. You are not rejecting an individual; you are rejecting a request. Also, while you are saying no, make arrangements to get together on another occasion when you actually have time.

- Be loyal to you: Remember the discussion regarding self-love and boundaries? Ensure that your own morals and values are not compromised whenever you say yes. Be sincere with yourself; do you really want to do this?

Stress, exhaustion, and irritability result from the inability to say no. The ability to say no fosters inner serenity, self-awareness, and regard. Spend time evaluating yourself and your needs to develop and recover from narcissistic abuse rather than obsessing over saying no. In addition to enjoying your leisure time, make time for family and supportive peers for the sake of your sanity.

Setting Limits with Narcissists

The sole purpose and insight of a narcissist is to be in complete control, resulting in a lack of stringent limits in their own life. Due to issues with low self-esteem and an abundance of insecurities, they resent or covet those who set limits. It would be a waste of time for them to attempt to gain access to the confident person's thoughts. In order to reclaim your life and sanity from the narcissist, it is crucial that you immediately establish these boundaries as a protective barrier between you and those who assaulted you. So, how do you specifically set boundaries with narcissists? How it works:

1. Be aware of the limit

Consider your values, which may include placing your family first, not abusing animals, being vegan or vegetarian, having respect, etc. Focus on what you are willing to accept and what you are not during this process. You may be unwilling to accept any form of control or negative influences, for instance. One way to set clear boundaries is to inform the narcissist that you will exit the conversation until they respect your values if they continue to blackmail, gaslight, or control your actions. Since you have already issued the initial warning, you must reiterate it if the behavior persists and then leave the area immediately after. Thus, the conflict will not escalate, and you will feel better about yourself for not engaging. When you know where the line is, you can feel confident, calm, and stronger.

2.Have an escape plan

Everyone is permitted to defend their own liberties. Therefore, if you need to flee a dangerous situation, you should be prepared to do so. You need no permission to depart. Simply do it. You have the ability to recognize disrespectful behavior and remove yourself from it at any time, whether you need to make an excuse to exit or you need a supportive friend to do so on your behalf. You could also set an alarm on your phone prior to the engagement, then use the alarm as an excuse to accept the call, regardless of whether there is an actual call. This will stall the situation and give you time to initiate a conversation about how you need to depart — no explanation required.

3. There is no need for clarification.

Typically, in a narcissistic interaction, you will be interrogated with a series of potentially irrelevant inquiries. When asked questions like "How do you spend your money? Where are you relocating? Why are you so occupied? You can respond, "That is my private information, and I do not wish to share it." Afterwards, they may call you out and make you feel remorseful for not sharing, but the less they know, the less leverage they have over you in the future. When they persist in being impolite, as they undoubtedly will, refer back to rule number one: where to draw the line.

4. Describe their abusive method

Narcissists are not masters of their emotions, thoughts, and actions, as is the case with NPD; however, you can still point out their mistakes. They may perceive it as playing the "blame game," but in reality, you are laying the groundwork to avoid being abused. For instance, when someone says, "You'll get what you deserve," you can respond, "I feel like that was a passive-aggressive insult based on how they've said it in the past." Even if they refute it (which they will), you have enough faith in yourself to know what is occurring in this moment. You can also inform them that you have observed them interrupting you every time you attempt to speak. Make them conscious of their actions and provide them with the option to cease. Alternatively, revert back to rule number one.

5.Redirect the attention to yourself

After they have interrupted you, alert them with confidence. You can then redirect the focus to your original statement. Occasionally, however, it is best to simply walk away, because you know in your heart whether they are actively listening or merely listening to respond and speak about themselves, as is their custom. In order to avoid becoming a victim of their social abuse or passive aggression, check in with yourself to determine how you are feeling. If you do not check in with yourself, you may act on your impulses and engage in the narcissist's behavior, which will only exacerbate the conflict and give the narcissist the upper hand.

6.Be ready to perform this action more than once.

The only person narcissists consider is themselves, so forget about yourself and the initial boundaries you have established. Perhaps they have not forgotten, but they simply do not care. Reiterating your boundaries or reminding them of your boundaries is a process you will need to complete each time.

7. Remember self-love

Self-love includes knowing when to walk away and when one is being disrespected. The most effective method to maintain your self-love is to recall the years of control they exerted over you as a child. Realize that if you succumb to their charm and persuasion, you will once again be subjected to incessant abuse. Yes, they can change, but they must first desire to change.

8.Focus on your spiritual development

Continuously focusing on yourself and your personal development is one of the most essential steps to take. When a narcissist observes that you are working on yourself and will no longer tolerate their abuse, they will back off because they will feel incompetent toward you and begrudge your personal development. Several questions to ask yourself in order to remain on course are: What do I stand for? Do I wish to engage while feeling inferior or incompetent? What is the greatest resolution I can make right now? Your obvious responses should relate to becoming the person you've always desired to be and obtaining self-respect. Keeping this in mind will allow you to escape their reality and build a solid foundation for yourself.

Consequences are always the result of imposing rigorous limitations.

Don't be concerned about disappointing them or hurting their emotions. Again, narcissists only consider themselves and their own struggles. They use your difficulties to hinder your progress. Be aware that your boundaries will have consequences for your and their actions when you establish them. For instance, if the narcissist chooses to project their emotions onto you, you can either walk away to defuse the situation or confront the narcissist in the moment. Furthermore, no explanation is required.

A narcissist is analogous to an adult child, so you must enforce your boundaries or they will exploit you at the first opportunity.

How Should I Approach the Narcissist in My Relationship?

Having an intimate relationship with a person with narcissistic personality disorder can be difficult. It can also be extremely distressing at times.

As a malady of the mind, narcissistic personality disorder (NPD) may manifest uniquely in each individual.

Some individuals may experience less severe symptoms and are able to maintain long-term relationships.

Others may have developed protective mechanisms that lead them to manipulate their spouses, friends, and family members.

NPD is never a matter of personal choice. It is not evidence that a person is a "bad person."

What is referred to as "problematic behaviors" is a set of symptoms of a disorder that can cause immense suffering and alter a person's perception of herself and others.

On the other hand, being on the receiving end of callous behavior can negatively impact your physical and mental health.

HOW CAN A RELATIONSHIP TOLERATE NARCISSISTIC CHARACTERISTICS?.

A narcissistic personality disorder is an issue of mental health.

NPD is one of 10 personality disorders characterized by low self-esteem, a desire for admiration, a lack of empathy, and a preoccupation with oneself.

It is estimated that between 0.5% and 5% of the U.S. population may be affected by this mental health condition. It is a more prevalent reliable source among men.

Narcissism is a disorder in which individuals struggle to maintain realistic and stable self-esteem.

"Individuals with extreme narcissism typically have trouble recognizing that other people have emotions, and they frequently prioritize their own desires over the needs, feelings, and rights of others," he adds.

The Diagnostic and Statistical Manual of Mental Disorders (DSM-5) states that at least five of the following nine symptoms must be present on a consistent basis in order to diagnose non-affective personality disorder.

a grandiose sense of self-importance preoccupation with illusions of infinite prosperity, power, genius, or perfect love perception that they are "special" and unique need for excessive admiration sense of entitlement interpersonal manipulation strategies to achieve their goals

A lack of empathy behavior and attitudes that are condescending and haughty.

Not everyone with NPD will experience these symptoms to the same degree or to the same extent.

Moreover, a narcissistic personality encompasses more than a scattering of behaviors or attitudes. Only a specialist in mental health can correctly diagnose the disorder.

Also, anyone may exhibit any of these behaviors at some point. This does not suggest they have a personality disorder.

You may, for instance, desire praise and appreciation from specific individuals, or you may employ manipulative techniques in your interactions. This alone does not indicate the presence of the condition.

Understanding that narcissistic personality is a disorder of mental health and not a personal choice is crucial. However, this does not imply that you must tolerate being handled in a way that could cause you harm.

The majority of people with the illness are unaware of how they behave or the potential consequences of their actions on others. It is part of the complexity of the condition.

This is essential knowledge because it can help you recognize that endeavoring to "change" someone or "show" them their wrongdoings is not always effective.

In some instances, calling someone out on their actions may result in anger and vindictive behavior.

It is essential to recognize that narcissism occurs on a spectrum. Not all forms of narcissistic dysfunction are equally destructive to healthy relationships.

Regardless of the situation, you must develop coping strategies that prevent you from becoming injured.

Learn about narcissistic personality disorder.

Understanding the illness is one of the best ways to protect yourself from the emotional distress of being in a relationship with a narcissist.

Understanding the symptoms and complexities of NPD may help you develop empathy for your partner, but you should avoid mistaking anything they do or say as "personal."

In fact, understanding NPD may enable you to depersonalize insults, criticisms, and other destructive behaviors.

Maintaining a relationship with someone who has a narcissistic personality requires recognizing that it is not about you, but rather their own mental health issue.

2. Do not romanticize your partner

At times, individuals with NPD may be endearing, engaging, and confident. Consequently, their attitude and vitality may attract others.

As with any other relationship, it is essential to view the other person as they truly are, including their less-than-charming qualities.

This means that you may want to observe how they treat other people, how they discuss past relationships, and how they behave with you when they are dissatisfied.

It is essential to have reasonable expectations for what you can obtain from your relationship. This also includes not defending their actions if they offend you.

Clearly describe how their conduct affects you

Since people with NPD are less likely to be aware of how their actions affect you, it is imperative that you express your concerns.

Remaining mute for the sake of "keeping the peace" could ultimately work against you.

When a person lives with NPD, any criticism, even moderate ones, may irritate them. It is also essential to anticipate a hostile response or defensive stance when communicating with them.

Protecting oneself from narcissistic abuse entails preventing others from degrading, minimizing, or trampling one's genuine ideas and emotions.

Occasionally, a simple, firm statement such as "Hey, my feelings are important, and I don't believe you are listening to them or taking them seriously" is sufficient.

4. Set distinct boundaries

Some individuals with NPD may believe they have the right to invade every aspect of your existence.

According to their perspective, your primary life goal may be to satisfy their needs. They may not fully appreciate that you have your own desires.

Setting boundaries may be crucial for maintaining a healthy relationship.

When dealing with a person who is acting inappropriately, I would recommend establishing clear boundaries through straightforward communication and being prepared to walk away if the other person does not respect your boundaries.

In addition, it is essential to clearly define these boundaries and recognize when they are disregarded or questioned.

Perhaps your lover constantly texts or calls you while you are out with friends in an effort to get your attention. They may even become extremely enraged and accuse you of ignoring their needs at the time.

Consequently, it is essential to articulate your boundaries.

You could respond by saying, "I'm busy, and I'll get back to you when I can." You could also be more specific and say, "Please do not interrupt me when I am spending time with my friends or family."

Anticipate criticism, but strive to maintain your composure.

5. Do not accept negative comments

Developing thick skin is certainly simpler said than done. Some people are naturally more sensitive than others, and it can be difficult not to let severe actions affect you.

It is essential to recognize that their actions are not a reflection of you. They are symptoms of a personality disorder.

Taking criticisms and remarks personally can quickly erode one's confidence and sense of self-worth.

Developing a thicker epidermis may assist you in maintaining a healthy sense of self and reasonable expectations for your relationship.

However, this does not imply ignoring inappropriate behavior. Even if they suffer from a mental illness, they do not have the right to repeatedly abuse or belittle you.

6. Establish a support system

In certain circumstances, a spouse with NPD may not provide the necessary support and attention.

Developing new friendships and maintaining current relationships may help you find emotional fulfillment outside of your relationship.

Some individuals with NPD may attempt to isolate you. They may endeavor to retain power and control, thereby commanding your constant attention.

This may make maintaining other relationships difficult at best.

However, recognize that you require attention and assistance as well. If you're not getting what you need from the relationship, you have the right to look elsewhere.

7. Consult a counsellor

Whether or not your spouse is receiving therapy for their mental health issue, it may be prudent for you to consult with a therapist.

In addition to assisting you understand and appreciate the narcissistic personality of your partner, a therapist may provide guidance and support.

A therapist might remind you to prioritize yourself, even if your spouse is sending you plain or subtle signals that your needs are unimportant.

A specialist in mental health can also assist you in recognizing when your partner employs manipulation techniques or other narcissistic methods, and when this behavior crosses the line into abuse.

If you choose to depart, make preparations beforehand.

Leaving a relationship with a person with NPD can be exceedingly challenging.

Some individuals with NPD may have difficulty allowing you go without attempting to re-engage you. In other situations, they may also wish to have the final say.

Whether someone is questioning your discernment or making you feel guilty about leaving, it is essential to remember why you made the decision.

In addition, it may be essential to plan ahead and provide explicit reasons for quitting.

Though it may appear to be an effective method for addressing undesirable behavior, threatening to depart and then not following through may backfire.

It may grant them more authority and imply that they do not need to change.

Consider announcing your departure only when you are truly prepared to do so.

There are times when it can be advantageous to sever all ties with a person or group, as they may attempt to woo you back. They may also abruptly end the relationship and treat you with hostility.

When it is time to depart

Relationship termination is always difficult. Even if your spouse's NPD has harmed you greatly, you may still have a great deal of affection for them.

When behavior escalates to mental or physical abuse, however, it is time to depart.

Occasionally, you must determine whether or not the connection is likely to strengthen.

When someone acts aggressively or threatens violence, it's time to flee.

ADDITIONAL SIGNS THAT IT MAY BE TIME TO SEPARATE - when your partner consistently fails to comprehend your emotions and engages in:

psychological assault

verbal abuse

physical violence

sexual harassment

Or, if you have a strong intuitive feeling that the relationship is toxic and will continue to be so, it may also be time to part ways.

This includes a sense of isolation from peers and family

Having difficulty enjoying activities Feeling afraid to be yourself or behave in a certain manner around your partner Questioning your self-worth frequently feeling remorseful about expressing your opinions and desires

A narcissist can change?

It is simple to maintain hope that your spouse will change or outgrow their narcissistic personality.

Research indicates that certain narcissistic traits may diminish with age.

Long-term psychotherapy may also be effective in treating NPD, according to a reliable source. However, few individuals with the illness seek professional assistance.

However, if they desire therapy, praising and supporting their decision may encourage them to continue treatment.

Change is generally a slow and gradual process that requires time, but it is possible.

Let's conclude

Relationships with individuals with narcissistic personalities can be challenging.

In certain instances, the behavior of a person with the disease may be disagreeable and aggressive, despite not being the result of a deliberate choice.

The persistent desire for praise, the lack of empathy, and the use of manipulative methods may hinder your relationship with a person with NPD.

This is why it is essential to establish clear boundaries and develop alternative strategies for dealing with their efforts to exert control.

At times, it can be difficult to determine where deceptive behavior ends and maltreatment begins.

If you believe you are in a relationship with someone who exhibits narcissistic characteristics, you may wish to consult a mental health professional.

www.ingramcontent.com/pod-product-compliance
Lightning Source LLC
Chambersburg PA
CBHW050357120526
44590CB00015B/1730